Rookie

Biography

D1498931

LUDWIG VAN
BEETHOVEN
A Revolutionary Composer

by Joanne Mattern

Content Consultant
Nanci R. Vargus, Ed.D.
Professor Emeritus, University of Indianapolis

Reading Consultant
Jeanne M. Clidas, Ph.D.
Reading Specialist

Children's Press®
An Imprint of Scholastic Inc.

Library of Congress Cataloging-in-Publication Data
Names: Mattern, Joanne, 1963- author.
Title: Ludwig van Beethoven: a revolutionary composer/by Joanne Mattern.
Description: New York : Children's Press, 2017. | Series: Rookie biographies | Includes index.
Identifiers: LCCN 2016030327| ISBN 9780531222898 (library binding)
| ISBN 9780531227701 (pbk.)
Subjects: LCSH: Beethoven, Ludwig van, 1770-1827–Juvenile literature. | Composers–Austria–
Biography–Juvenile literature.
Classification: LCC ML3930.B4 M39 2017 | DDC 780.92 [B] –dc23
LC record available at https://lccn.loc.gov/2016030327

Produced by Spooky Cheetah Press
Design by Judith Christ-Lafond
Poem by Jodie Shepherd

Photos ©: cover Beethoven: UniversalImagesGroup/Getty Images; cover background, back
cover: Paha_L/iStockphoto; 3: Erin Cadigan/Thinkstock; 4: Ralf Hettler/iStockphoto; 7 inset:
imageBROKER/Superstock, Inc.; 8: akg-images/The Image Works; 9: Irene Abdou/Alamy Images;
11: Lebrecht Music & Arts/The Image Works; 12: Fine Art Images/Heritage/The Image Works;
14-15: Lebrecht Music and Arts Photo Library/Alamy Images; 16-17: Imagno/Wien Museum/
The Image Works; 18: Beethoven-Haus Bonn; 19: INTERFOTO/Alamy Images; 20: jianying yin/
iStockphoto; 22: Lebrecht Music & Arts/The Image Works; 23: Mary Evans Picture Library/
The Image Works; 24-25: AF archive/Alamy Images; 26: INTERFOTO/Alamy Images; 29: Robert
Huberman/Superstock, Inc.; 30: Erin Cadigan/Thinkstock; 31 top: Robert Huberman/Superstock,
Inc.; 31 center top: Irene Abdou/Alamy Images; 31 center bottom: Rischgitz/Getty Images; 31
bottom: Bettmann/Getty Images; 32: Erin Cadigan/Thinkstock.

Maps by Mapping Specialists.

TABLE OF CONTENTS

Meet Ludwig van Beethoven

Ludwig van Beethoven (LOOD-vig VON BAY-toe-ven) was one of the greatest composers ever. He wrote **classical** music. Beethoven's music was loud and exciting. It was different from other music of the time. Beethoven's work changed music forever.

Ludwig van Beethoven was born in Bonn, Germany, on December 16, 1770.

Ludwig's father, Johann, was a singer. His mother took care of the house. She also looked after Ludwig and his two younger brothers.

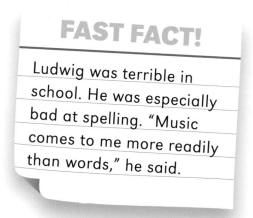

FAST FACT!

Ludwig was terrible in school. He was especially bad at spelling. "Music comes to me more readily than words," he said.

This is the house where Beethoven was born.

GERMANY

●Bonn

MAP KEY

● City where Beethoven was born

Area enlarged

Young Ludwig practices with his father.

When he was little, Ludwig learned to play the **clavier** and the violin. His father taught him. He was a very tough teacher. He made Ludwig practice for hours every day. If Ludwig made a mistake, his father beat him. He wanted Ludwig to be a famous musician.

A clavier is a keyboard instrument similar to a piano.

Ludwig's hard work soon paid off. He played in his first concert when he was just seven years old! But his father said he was only six. He lied to make Ludwig's talent seem even more shocking. His father did not need to lie. It was amazing that a little boy could play such beautiful music.

FAST FACT!

Because of his father's lie, Ludwig always thought he was younger than he really was.

This is a picture of Beethoven's father.

11

Prince Maximilian Franz

Ludwig also composed, or wrote, music. He published his first work when he was 12 years old. At 14 years old, Ludwig became the organist at the court of the prince of Austria. His name was Prince Maximilian Franz.

Off to Vienna

When Beethoven was about 17, the prince sent him to Vienna, Austria, to study. Vienna was the center of music. Beethoven was there for only a few weeks when he found out his mother was very sick. He rushed home to be with her when she died.

This painting shows Beethoven playing in Vienna.

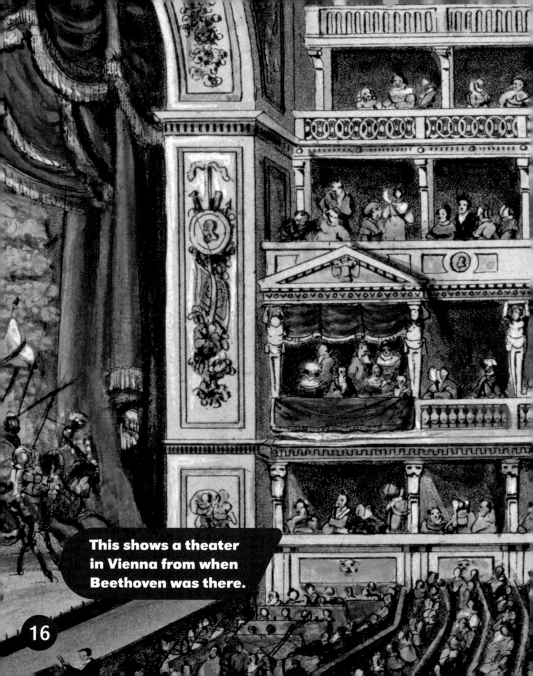

This shows a theater in Vienna from when Beethoven was there.

Beethoven returned to Vienna in 1792. He presented his First **Symphony** at a concert in 1800. The long piece of music was loud and forceful. People were shocked when they heard it. They were used to quieter music. Still, everyone said the symphony was a masterpiece.

FAST FACT!

Later, Beethoven did not like his First Symphony. He felt his music got better as he grew older.

Sadness and Triumph

When he was in his late 20s, Beethoven realized he was losing his hearing. This was a terrible thing to happen to a musician! Beethoven was very upset. Still, he continued to write and perform music.

Beethoven used this ear trumpet to help him hear.

Even beginners
can play some
Beethoven songs!

Between 1803 and 1811, Beethoven wrote some of his best and most famous music. Not all of Beethoven's music was loud and complicated. Beethoven also wrote fun pieces. Many piano students around the world learn Beethoven's song "Für Elise."

FAST FACT!

As he grew older, Beethoven became grouchy. He could be hard to get along with. However, people were fond of him. He had many friends.

The Ninth Symphony

Beethoven's hearing got worse as he got older. In 1811, he had to stop playing in public. He could not **conduct** his own work either. By 1814, Beethoven was almost completely deaf. But he still heard music in his head, and he kept composing.

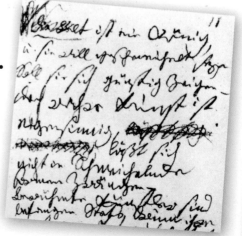

After Beethoven went deaf, he used notes like this one to communicate with his friends.

Sometimes Beethoven's work was inspired by nature.

In 1824, Beethoven completed his Ninth Symphony. Many people think it is the greatest piece of music he ever wrote. On May 7, Beethoven made a rare public appearance to help conduct the symphony.

He could not hear the audience cheering. One of the singers turned him to face the audience so he could see them clapping. Beethoven was so happy, he started to cry.

FAST FACT!

If you have ever seen a *Peanuts* movie or TV special, you have probably heard Beethoven's music. Schroeder loves to play Beethoven's works on his piano.

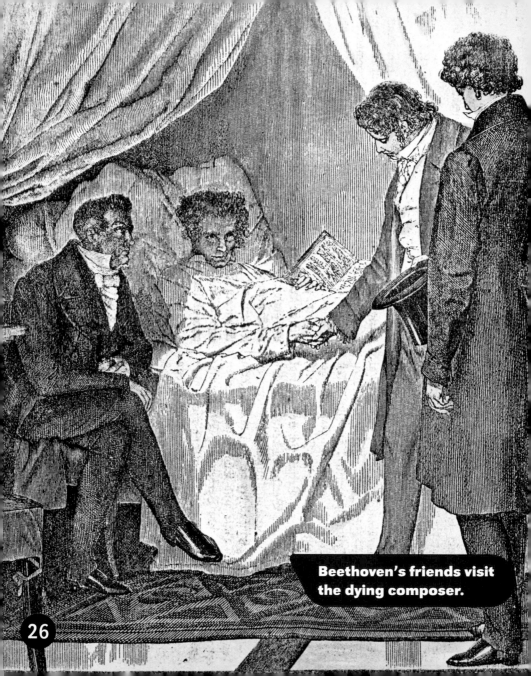

Beethoven's friends visit the dying composer.

In 1826, Beethoven caught a bad cold. He became very sick. On March 26, 1827, in the middle of a terrible storm, Beethoven died at home.
He was 56 years old.
Several friends were at his side. There was a huge crash of thunder as he died.

FAST FACT!

About 20,000 people went to Beethoven's funeral.

Today we remember Beethoven as one of the greatest composers who ever lived. His music was full of strong emotions. Although he had a difficult life, his music still makes people happy today.

Timeline of Beethoven's Life

1770	1778	1787
Born on December 16	Performs his first public concert	Goes to Vienna for the first time

Writes his First Symphony; begins to lose his hearing

Dies on March 26

1792 > **1800** > **1814** > **1827**

Moves to Vienna

Becomes totally deaf

A Poem About Ludwig van Beethoven

His music was loud and exciting.
His symphonies had plenty of spirit.
When he went deaf, he kept writing music
but was never able to hear it.

You Can Be an Innovator

 Do not be afraid to try new things!

Do something familiar in a different way.

Enjoy the unexpected! Allow your
imagination to create something new.

Glossary

- **classical** (KLAS-ih-kuhl): style of music popular between 1750 and 1830

- **clavier** (KLAH-veer): early instrument with a keyboard, like a piano

- **conduct** (kuhn-DUHKT): direct a group of musicians as they sing or play

- **symphony** (SIM-fun-nee): long piece of music written for a full orchestra, usually consisting of several parts

Index

Facts for Now

Visit this Scholastic Web site for more information on
Ludwig van Beethoven and download the Teaching Guide for this series:
www.factsfornow.scholastic.com
Enter the keywords Ludwig van Beethoven

About the Author

Joanne Mattern has written more than 250 books for children. She especially likes writing biographies because she loves to learn about real people and the things they do. Joanne also plays piano and sings, and Beethoven is one of her favorite composers. She grew up in New York State and still lives there with her husband, four children, and several pets.